DEPRESSION IS CURABLE!

Important information about the medical treatment of depression in adolescents, adults, PMS, and the elderly.

BY DR. COREY ERICKSEN

Rainbow Press P.O. Box 855 Clackamas, OR 97015

EDITED BY VICTORIA FAIRHAM
ILLUSTRATIONS BY ANNE MAERTENS
COVER DESIGN BY CHARLES J. KARL III

First Printing June 1986

ISBN # 0-9610156-1-6

Rainbow Press
Clackamas, Oregon

ACKNOWLEDGEMENT

I give special thanks to my wife, Laurie, who first recognized the need for a book such as this. Her ever-present support and encouragement made this book a reality.

Retired nurse, Vivian Anderson, first brought to my attention the gravity and prevalance of depression. I thank her for her selfless service, both to help depressed people and to educate the public.

I also thank Jo Ann Blanchard, my publisher and agent, for her enthusiastic support, and for her dedication to the idea of treating those suffering from depression.

CONTENTS

ABOUT THE AUTHOR

Dr. Corey Ericksen is a Family Practice Physician. He is Board certified by the American Academy of Family Practice. Dr. Ericksen is a member of the Utah State Licensing Board and a diplomat of the American College of Family Practice. He is married to Laurie Anderson and they have four children.

INTRODUCTION

Most physicians, regardless of their training or specialty, develop special interests within the field of medicine. My interest in depression was sparked by a nurse, Vivian Anderson, who had searched for information and answers about depression on behalf of family and friends. Once I became aware of the potential devastation of this illness, I began researching it on my own. Then, when treating my patients, I began to look for the symptoms of depression with a much greater degree of sensitivity and knowledge. Although I have never had chemical depression myself, I feel I have had enough experience with those who have, to allow me to understand the terrible anguish they experience.

I have seen countless numbers of people suffer needlessly from the symptoms of depression; people who have lost months or years of their lives to depression. I have witnessed divorces and suicide attempts as a result of depression.

On the positive side, in the course of treatment, I have watched the miracle of medicine transform anxious, irritable and withdrawn patients to calm and kind persons that existed before depression struck.

Although the average length of an untreated depression is about six months, I have talked with people who have had it for years and had forgotten what it was like to be normal. My heart has gone out for those people who have experienced a terrible, unexplained change destroy their character, their careers, and their families. As I started treating more and more patients for depression, I searched for literature they and their family members could read in order to better understand depression as an illness.

After unsucessfully searching for a single source of written information that was both concise and easy to understand on the subject, I became determined to write this book, so that people could use it in their attempt to understand depression.

Sometimes people who are being treated for depression need something concrete to show their family and friends, in order to say, "See, it's not just in my head; I'm not crazy. It's physical, real, and it is a common problem."

I also wanted something that people unknowingly suffering from depression could pick up, read and then say, "Ah, hah! That's me! There is a name for what's been bothering me, and furthermore, there is a cure."

I wanted a reference book for counselors and ministers, for employers and spouses, for parents and for friends, so they could help those depressed, who might not be able to help themselves.

Science has made great strides in understanding and treating depression. Unfortunately, education of the public has lagged. Depression afflicts about one in every five people at some time in their lives. It will be a needless tragedy if any of these people fall into the never-diagnosed and untreated category. I hope this book makes a contribution in the fight against the common, yet misunderstood, illness we call depression.

CHAPTER ONE
It Can Happen To Anyone

Depression is one of the most common medical illnesses of our time, and yet it remains one of the most misunderstood. It is estimated that as many as one out of every five people will suffer a major episode of depression at some time in their life. Depression is a medical illness as real as high blood pressure or diabetes. It is a result of an actual imbalance of neurotransmitters, which are chemicals needed to transmit messages from the brain. This imbalance causes real and physical symptoms. It is not a disease of the mind, and people with this problem are not "crazy." It is felt in the medical field that depression is the physiologic, or physical, response to stress. That's all. It's not a curse or an irreversible condition that lasts forever. It is a physical, mental and emotional phenomenon that can be treated successfully with specific medicines.

When present, depression is a devastating condition, causing agony, only truly understood by those who have had the disease. Furthermore, it is a malady made worse by a number of factors, including stress. We have learned a great deal about depression in recent years. Unfortunately, widespread public education has not occurred in this area, and thousands of people suffer needlessly because they don't recognize the symptoms as treatable in relation to depression as an illness.

The symptoms of depression are sleep disturbances, irritability, failure to concentrate, and inability to accomplish tasks, changes in appetite with weight loss or weight gain, fatigue, decreased sexual interest, inability to enjoy doing things, physical complaints like backache, headache, etc., an overwhelmed feeling, often a feeling that life is not worth living, and strong feelings of inadequacy or lowered self-esteem. One does not have to have all of these symptoms to meet the diagnosis of depression, but a person should have at least four symptoms which have been present for at least two weeks and that interfere with the person's normal lifestyle. Because it is treatable, it is not only sad, but unjust, to know thousands of people suffer needlessly from depression.

Depression is a major cause of unhappy homes and unfulfilled lives. Not only does it change peoples' moods; it can change their personalities and their entire lives. Depression causes decreased work productivity, and is responsible for thousands of lost work hours.[1] It is a leading cause of spouse and child abuse. Some estimate depression to be associated with nearly half of all divorces and suicides.[2] Those suffering from depression experience frustration as an 'unknown power' causing anxiety, lowering self-esteem and dulling the ability to enjoy life. They recognize a dramatic change occurring in their lives, but have no explanation for the cause. They want to rid themselves of the inner turmoil, but the ability to do so is absent.

Husbands wonder what happened to the woman they married; wives wonder how their husband got

[1] C.A.H. Watts, O.B.E., "Depressive Disorders in the Community," *Journal of Clinical Psychiatry,* VL(1984), 70-77.

[2] Brisco & Smith, "Depression and Marital Turmoil," *Archives of General Psychiatry,* XIX (1973)811-817.
Barracloug Bunch, "100 Cases of Suicide," *British Journal of Psychiatry,* CXXV(1974),355.

out of control. Spouses are confused at the Jeckel and Hyde personality. Couples wonder what happened to their happy marriage, and children fall victim to irritable, desperate, or despondent parents.

Adolescents also suffer from depression. They may find their grades dropping; they develop negative interpersonal relationships, and lose friends. They may find coping with school and home activities and responsibilities too much to handle. They may withdraw from others and their normal activities.

Young children also can become depressed and suffer similar symptoms. A child of any age may send out signals for help in dealing with depression by complaining of headaches, stomachaches, or leg cramps with no apparent cause. They may have raging temper tantrums for no justifiable reason, or they may show signs of self-destruction.

Depression is also evident in the elderly. Memory loss, confused thinking and apathy are often attributed to senility, but may be caused by depression. Diagnosis is more difficult in this population, because similar symptoms may also be caused by inadequate diet, medications, loneliness or other health problems.

Is it Depression or the Blues?

When we speak here of depression, we are referring to a chemical imbalance called unipolar or "true chemical depression." This should not be confused with temporary feelings of unhappiness that everyone has experienced. All of us, at times, have emotional letdowns that occur during various times of the year, and often during holidays. Most of the time, when a person feels down, he or she is able to recognize a cause, for instance, a job related frustration, a friend moving away, or the car getting dented. These things can and do happen to everyone at one time or another. When these things happen, it is known that the unhappiness will pass. The person is able to function normally because when he knows it's temporary, it is easier to cope. But even if the person can't exactly identify the cause of the blues he still has life in perspective, and sees the positive side of things. Even though one is upset, he still realizes he will have other, maybe even better, job opportunities, find other friends, or get the car repaired. Life goes on. People compensate.

The blues come and go, but true chemical depression is continuous. There is a constant cloud over the affected person, about which nothing can be done. There is often an overwhelming feeling of helplessness, a heavy feeling that seems to darken the whole world. With true chemical depression, the positives, just don't seem to count. A promotion, a vacation, or any success does not help to lighten this heavy, dark feeling.

It is natural to become depressed in varying degrees as a response to the loss of a loved one, general problems, disappointments or other life crises. These are painful and difficult times for people, but these episodes of sadness and grief are normal and are temporary reactions to life's stresses. Time heals; the mood returns to normal, and people are able to function much as they did previously. A person who has true chemical depression, however, will have symptoms which do not resolve in a normal amount of time, and the person will not be able to function successfully.

Three Cases of Depression

Let me show you how depression affects the lives of so many people. The following stories represent typical examples of depression. None of them are actual histories based on any individual patient.

Carl and Sue had been married 18 years. They had four children. Carl had a stable income which was adequate for their needs. They had what everyone would have considered an ideal marriage. They themselves thought it was ideal — that is, until things started going downhill. There was no single event, no catastrophe, nothing they could think of that started the deterioration of Sue's ability to manage her home and her state of mind.

She began having difficulty falling asleep at night and felt very tired during the day. She blamed her tiredness on not sleeping well and assumed the problem was related to having "so much on her mind." It was a different sort of tired feeling. She felt like she would like to go back to bed and sleep, but there was something more to it, than only fatigue. It felt to her like a huge task to get even the simplest chores completed around the house. Her immaculate housekeeping became a matter of "just getting by." As the laundry stacked up she felt overwhelmed.

It was when she stopped getting up in the morning to fix breakfast for the family, that Carl first noticed something was definitely wrong. At first he was sympathetic. He tried harder to help around the house. He would give Sue time during the day to take a nap and send her to bed early. For two weeks he told her to stay in bed in the morning while he fixed breakfast and got the children off to school.

After a few weeks they both agreed that she must be sick. They visited their doctor, and a physical exam revealed nothing wrong. They were told it was probably a virus, and that she should be feeling better soon. A month passed and, instead of things getting better, things were getting worse.

Sue was feeling guilty about not being able to keep up with her responsibilities. She became irritable and things that had previously been of little consequence to her, suddenly became a "a big deal." The children slamming the door would cause her to scream at them. When Carl's work made him late for dinner, she became so upset she would say things they both knew she did not mean.

Carl began to lose his sympathy. They began arguing over everything, and he would find excuses to delay coming home at night. The children, partially neglected and becoming objects of tension, became more disagreeable and created more problems. Everyone sat at the dinner table in silence. There were no longer any family activities, and there existed a constant feeling of tension in the home.

When Carl would soften and offer to take Sue out for dinner or to the movies, she would either be too tired or just not feel like going. It seemed that Carl and Sue were drifting farther and farther apart, and Sue was entering her own little world. She would rather be by herself. She slept about fourteen hours a day and would frequently just sit down and cry.

Again Sue sought medical help on her own. She knew she could not go on like this. In the process of a thorough work-up she was tested for anemia and low blood sugar. Her thyroid function was studied, x-rays were taken, and blood drawn. She had a complete and expensive work-up, but all the findings were normal.

Sue felt like she had become a different person. Carl was convinced she was a different person. He even went so far as to accuse her of using drugs. Their situation deteriorated, and Carl suggested a divorce.

Sue knew that something inside was screaming at her to start shaping up, to get back on her feet, to get involved, to become once again the wife and mother she had been. She knew inside, that she did not want a divorce, and that she only wanted to have things back to normal again, but somehow the necessary energy and will were not there. Everything seemed hopeless. She just did not care anymore . . . . about anything.

* * * * * * * *

Jack was vice-president of sales for a large distributing corporation. His colleagues envied his position. He had his own office, private secretary, expense account, etc.. Rumor had it that he was the person to take over the regional sales office in the next promotion. His wall was covered with recognition awards. Jack seemed to have everything going for him.

Just two days before Christmas, when the custodian unlocked the offices for routine cleaning, he found Jack lying on the floor. A pool of dried blood stained the carpet beneath his head, and the gun remained in his hand. Jack's suicide was a great shock to everyone. That is, to everyone except those who had been closely associated with him during the previous months.

Four months earlier, Jack's wife was the first one who noticed changes in her husband's behavior. Jack was more anxious. He couldn't sit still. He always had to be doing something, and he doubled the number of cigarettes he was smoking. She frequently awakened at night to find Jack out of bed and either pacing around the house, or trying to work on his sales projections. She thought this was due to added stress at work and his efforts to earn a promotion.

Dan, an associate at work, soon noticed that Jack was turning into a workaholic. He would come in early and leave late. He no longer went out to lunch with the sales personnel, and he refused to stop off after work to have a drink or relax. This was not like Jack at all. Despite all the pressures he had experienced before, he always had taken things in stride. Jack lost his sense of humor and began snapping at the salesmen who did not meet their quotas. He began isolating himself and staying in the office more. He forgot appointments, and seemed very unlike the sharp businessman Dan had known so well. At times, it was as though Jack had lost his will to go on.

His wife started getting even more concerned when Jack lost his appetite and began losing weight. She too, noticed he was more quick tempered. They hadn't been to bed together for weeks. When she asked him to see a doctor, he reassured her that he was fine, and that he was just under a little more stress than usual at the office.

No one had suspected that Jack would consider killing himself. But it happened.

* * * * * * * * *

Lisa was a twenty-six-year-old mother of two, who had recently became the mother of three. Except for the usual adjustment problems of having babies, Lisa hadn't had any unusual difficulties coping as a mother. All three children were wanted and planned. There was no real financial strain on the family, and her husband, Ted, was very excited about finally getting a boy, after two girls.

Following the birth of the third baby, Lisa experienced "baby blues." It was manifested by the typical symptoms of frequent crying episodes over little things, some irritability and wanting to be left alone. She was overwhelmed thinking about all the work and responsibility that was going to be here as the mother of three children. Her friends told her that having two children was easy compared to adding a third one. That made her even more nervous.

The first two or three weeks at home went by without too many unusual problems; she received a lot of sympathetic help and understanding while she worked her way through the blues. Her mother who had come from Ohio to help after the baby was born, told her after three weeks though, that she needed to "snap out of it."

She stayed a week longer than planned, hoping it would help Lisa's frame of mind, but it did not. When her mother left, Lisa seemed to lose control. The blues got worse instead of better. Every little thing bothered her. She quit breast feeding because it became inconvenient. While she should have been dieting to get her excess weight off, she had a ravenous appetite and was gaining weight, not seeming to care.

Ted's sympathy turned to frustration, resentment, and then to anger. What had happened to their happy family? Lisa wanted to "snap out of it" but she just couldn't. When she would evaluate the situation, she realized what she needed to do. She needed to stop eating so much and lose weight, which would make her feel better about herself. She needed to get things done around the house. Maybe then she and Ted would stop arguing, and the children would start behaving better. Maybe she would feel like getting out of that seemingly dreary house and doing something. How she was going to do this she didn't know. It seemed like it was a vicious cycle, and she had no energy to stop any segment of it. She knew something was wrong. It seemed as though she had no control of her life anymore. She needed help; she wanted help, but she felt she had nowhere to turn.

* * * * * * * *

Each of the above stories represents thousands just like it occurring throughout the world. The frustrations experienced by those in these stories are typical of depressed persons and will be recognized by thousands of people as they read them. For those who have, or have had depression, no explanation of these symptoms is necessary. For the benefit of those who have not had depression let me try to describe it.

Progression of the Illness

The hallmark of depression is change. The former "life of the party" no longer goes out at night. The fireball employee loses his or her zeal. The ideal homemaker can't force herself to cook meals and do laundry, or the Thursday night bowler finds excuses to stay home. Furthermore, the changes persist.

There is also a change in personality as those who are depressed fall victim to mood changes and irritability. Nothing seems fun or even pleasurable anymore, and they would rather be by themselves. They recognize that stress worsens the problems, so they try to avoid responsibilities as much as possible, which reinforces their already present feelings of inadequacy and low self-esteem. They sense that something is terribly wrong inside, yet cannot understand it and seldom recognize it as depression. Because of the very nature of depression, an attitude of "I don't care" develops, and it becomes impossible to change this attitude without treatment.

Those affected, logically know what should be done, but cannot do it. For example, if they recognize they are losing weight, they know they should eat, but cannot force themselves to do so. They know they get mad and irritable at little things, but cannot help themselves. They understand they should not be tired because they already sleep more than they ever did, yet they can't make themselves do even the simplest of tasks.

This is interpreted as lacking ambition or being lazy or slothful, which leads to further feelings of guilt. They recognize they are not as capable as they used to be. Their mental acuity is decreased; their work production suffers drastically, and their family relationships deteriorate. They feel worthless or sinful, and these feelings are fertile ground in which doubt, guilt, lack of will, and low self-esteem may grow. Many victims give up trying.

As mental attempts to change things fail, the feelings of inadequacy and the frustration are reinforced. People who have been, or are depressed, describe this feeling as "like being in a deep, dark hole, and frantically trying to get out, but just digging the hole deeper and deeper." It's like being in a tunnel with no light at the end. They suffer needlessly, not recognizing that their tiredness, their hopeless feelings, sleep disturbance, irritability, etc., are symptoms of an underlying chemical depression.

Because depression presents itself with a wide range of symptoms, people do not usually associate these as a single medical problem. In general, people do not understand depression. In a recent poll, I asked

PACKING S

1 4 9 9

Via

Ship To

Market ID: 741756302
Order ID: 1499021
Order Date: 10/20/2026
Shipping Method:

ABE APTP Order
0000000000
help@textbookrush.com
800 AVONDALE AVE
JMZ8WMYD
COLUMBUS, OH 43212, US

SKU	QTY	TITLE	TO
BSM.1B6FK	1	Depression Is Curable!: Important Information About the Medical Treatment of Depression in Adolescents, Adults, Pms, and the Elderly	

Order Total: $11.87

Your order has been packaged and created with great care. Enjoy! Bay State Books

#1499021

many people to define depression. One out of every twenty-five really understood depression, and that was because they had been diagnosed and treated for it themselves. Some of the more common answers were: "It's when you feel blue and discouraged." "It's a feeling you often get after having a baby." "It's when you feel like crying all the time." "It's when you walk around with your head down and won't talk to anyone."

When asked to define the feelings or symptoms associated with depression, the general answer was an attempt to describe sadness or melancholia. Not one person out of twenty-four associated it with sleep disturbance or irritability, which are two of the most common symptoms. Giant strides have been made over the past years regarding diagnosis and treatment of depression. Unfortunately, the education of the public on this illness has not kept pace.

The Acceptance of Depression: Yesterday and Today

It wasn't too many years ago that people with symptoms of depression were considered "crazy" or "psychotic" and placed in mental institutions. One professional told me about her experiences as a nurse in a psychiatric diagnosis ward. Patients were admitted to this ward from a large county in California. For a two-week period of time, they were diagnosed. There was very little treatment in this clinic. Court was held, and patients were evaluated and diagnoses established. Often they were committed to state mental hospitals. The nurse remembered the frustrating feeling of inadequacy felt by health care personnel as they counseled with patients, judges, family members and clergy when these patients were judged unable to function in society. She saw many young mothers with newborn children that needed care, women going through menopause, young men with families to support, and older persons who had been productive all their lives. All had fallen victim to depression, and at that time there was no relief; institutionalization was the only option. All were victims of a physical illness, but the remedy and cure had not been discovered. Not only were their lives and those of their families disrupted, often permanently, but they carried the stigma of having a "mental illness."

Now we recognize depression as an actual chemical imbalance that will be explained in detail in chapter two. It is important for people to understand what true chemical depression is, and to realize that these individuals are not "crazy," that they are not "losing their minds," but that these symptoms are completely normal for someone suffering from depression. Depression needs to be accepted as a treatable medical illness.

Premenstrual syndrome, or PMS sometimes manifests itself as depression. In Europe, depression, as part of PMS has taken on legal significance. Three women were reported to have committed repeated criminal acts at monthly intervals, suggesting an imbalance of menstrual hormones. They responded to treatment with progesterone. As a consequence of this report, the courts in the United Kingdom and France now accept PMS as grounds for plea of temporary insanity.[3] This has become an issue in the United States and other countries.

Depression is not a new disease. It has been around as long as the common cold. It has plagued humankind since ancient times. Job, an Old Testament prophet of ancient days, was plagued with every malady known to man, including depression. After suffering for a long period of time over his many losses and ailments, he, in great despair, fell victim to what sounds like reactive depression. He even longed for death. Depression was one of the few recognized mental illnesses of ancient times. It was described

[3] Daniel H. Riddick N.D. P.H.D., "The Premenstrual Syndrome," *The Female Patient,* IIX(December 1983), 47.

with amazing accuracy by Hippocrates, the great Greek physician, and Galen of Rome. They describe the exact same illness that we are faced with today. A careful review of history reveals many well-known and great people who have suffered from depression. They include Vincent Van Gogh, Ernest Hemingway, and Sigmund Freud. Other great men, such as Abraham Lincoln, Theodore Roosevelt, Nathaniel Hawthorne and astronaut Buzz Aldrin have also been victims. Winston Churchill used to call it "my black dog."[4].

Even though the disease is old, our knowledge about it is relatively new. Just in the past few years we have gained insight into its cause and made progress toward treatment. It hasn't been very long ago, that people were placed in institutions for depression because they were not able to cope with life, while countless others just suffered with it undiagnosed. It has only been in the past twenty years or so, that depression has been dealt with by anyone other than psychiatrists.

We know that from ten to thirty percent of the population will have severe enough depression to require medication. Is the number rising or are we just diagnosing it better now?

The answer is probably both. Conditions of our time are conducive to anxiety and depression. Ours is the day of specialization. Our science, industry and professions are so complex and specialized that we are required to learn more and more, and perform better and better, just to keep up with technology. The progress of our day and age is traveling at an unprecedented pace that is constantly being accelerated. The world crowds in on us through our media, technology, and lifestyle until we eat and sleep, rest and work, travel and wait with schedule in hand.

[4] Donald W. McKen N.D., *Why Isn't Johnny Crying*' (W.W. Norton & Company, Inc.), P. 21.

Through it all, we have little or no time to sit down and organize our lives, to rest, to enjoy ourselves or to meditate.

On the other hand, health care providers are receiving more information on diagnosing depression, and people are becoming more aware of it, with increasing interest. Yet I feel we are still on the tip of the iceburg.

True chemical depression is a medical problem of mega-proportion. It affects from ten to thirty percent of all people directly, and millions more of their family members indirectly. It probably affects men and women equally; however, women are treated more frequently overall than men. It is possible women are more willing to seek help. The people suffering severe symptoms of depression in this country alone number in the millions, and the great majority of these go undiagnosed.

Depression is also an enormously significant social problem. It disrupts lives and ruins families. It is a major cause of suicide, divorce, job-related problems, spouse and child abuse.

Suicide has gone from the twenty-second highest cause of death in 1920 to the eighth or ninth highest cause in 1980. It is now estimated that one in every one hundred Americans has attempted to kill himself at one time. Approximately fifteen percent of severely depressed patients may ultimately die of suicide. Many studies show that of all people who have attempted suicide, more than half had depression. A study by Clarkin and others,[5] examined twenty-four adolescents and twenty adults who were hospitalized following serious suicide attempts. One hundred percent of the adults and seventy-one percent of the adolescents were suffering from major depressive disorder: depression.

[5] Michael Aronoff M.D., John Clarkin P.H.D., Ruth Corn M.S.W., Richard Friedman M.D., Stephen Hurt P.H.D., "Affective Character Pathology of Suicidal Adolescent and Young Adult Patients," *Journal of Clinical Psychiatry*, VL (1984), 19-22.

Another study of one hundred actual cases of suicide found that, in retrospect, the majority of them had visited their physician shortly before their suicide with symptoms of depression, but relatively few had received specific treatment.[6]

In many places the incidence of divorce is greater than fifty percent. This not only disrupts the lives of millions of men and women, but destroys security for the children involved. Many of the divorces are a direct effect of depression.

Instead of recognizing the symptoms of depression as part of a serious illness, these people are interpreted as lazy, bitchy, unproductive, cold and uncaring. Often personal appearance suffers, and the depressed person withdraws into a lonely shell. Arguments become frequent and often violent. It is no surprise that untreated depression frequently leads to divorce. In a study by Kathleen Merikangas, fifty-six married depressed patients were found to have a divorce rate nine times the expected rate for the population.[7] Another paper published by Brisco[8] showed that over half of the divorces studied, revealed at least one spouse was depressed before divorce proceedings began.

Depression is also one of the leading causes of spouse and child abuse. The hopelessness and despair brought about by depression are frequently signaled through physical abuse of self or others. In adolescents it can mean destructive delinquent behavior or even self-mutilation. In adults it can mean abuse by the distraught, depressed patient, or retaliation from the victim's spouse. Unfortunately, thousands of helpless children fall victim to anxious, irritable, and out-of-control depressed parents.

[6] Bunch. p. 133.

[7] Kathleen Ries Merikangas PHD, "Divorce and Assortive Mating Among Depressed Patients," *American Journal of Psychiatry* IXL(1984), 74-76.

[8] C.W. Brisco, J.B. Smith, E. Robins et al, "Divorce and Psychiatric Disease," *Archives of General Psychiatry*, XXIX(1973), 119.

The work force itself suffers greatly, however usually unknowingly. Depressed people cannot concentrate normally, they cannot force themselves to accomplish normal tasks, let alone surpass the expected. Countless numbers of promotions, and even jobs, are lost as a result of depression. One paper published estimated that the average time off work for the untreated patient was ten-and-a-half months.[9] Another study suggested a figure of eighteen months.[10] Multiply these lost months by the number of untreated working depressed people and the figure is staggering.

Depression is indeed a major medical and social problem. Fortunately we have come a long way in the understanding of depression. There is an effective treatment that can prevent millions of people from suffering needlessly from the symptoms of depression. We must now move forward with public education so people will recognize these symptoms and seek treatment. The next chapters will explain what causes depression and how it can be treated.

[9] C.A.H. Watts, "Depressive Disorders in the Community: The Scene in Great Britain," *Journal of Clinic Psychiatry,* VL(1984), 70-77.

[10] S.H. Kraines, *The Theory of Neuroses and Psychoses* (Philadelphia: Lea & Febiger, 1943.)

CHAPTER TWO
Understanding Depression

Depression is a complex group of conditions that manifests itself by many different symptoms. In the last chapter, I tried to describe the effects of the disease and how devastating it can be to normal living. Now I would like to define depression and explain what it is, and how it is diagnosed.

Perhaps it would be beneficial to define depression by its symptoms. To meet the criteria for depression one would need to have symptom number one, listed below, and any four other symptoms from the list. Furthermore, the symptoms should have been present for at least two weeks, and should be severe enough to interfere with the person's normal life style.

Symptoms of the Disease

1. Emotional instability (mood swings, irritability, anxiety and quick temper) When one is depressed, little things are bothersome that were never noticed before. Any small thing such as a neighbor dropping in, children slamming doors, a spouse being late or a baby crying can cause great anxiety which often results in some type of emotional outburst. He is more irritable, loses his temper easily, becomes argumentative, and has feelings of anger. This puts a great deal of stress on any family, causing discord and sometimes, eventually divorce. This is especially true when the spouse does not understand the reason for these changes. Usually the depressed person, no matter how strongly motivated by himself or others, cannot change this emotional instability with desire, threats or good advice.

Although both men and women may run the gamut of emotional reactions, women may often feel sad and have more frequent crying episodes for no reason, or at the slightest provocation. Men more often manifest their emotional crisis by withdrawing or showing fits of rage. Men too, may cry easily, but often try to hide this.

Found in all depression is some degree of anxiety (unusually strong apprehension about anything from work, to family, to abilities, etc.) Most anxieties have some component of depression. Despite the slow moving, slow thinking attitude, common in depression, there are usually feelings of anxiety that come and go, times when one wants to scream or "climb the wall." The depressed person may get uptight and nervous, or there may be just a subtle feeling inside that all is not well.

Emotional instability as discussed here may be cyclical in nature at a certain time in the female menstrual cycle. This may be a symptom of Premenstrual Syndrome (PMS) and is discussed at the end of this book.

2. Sleep Disturbance This occurs when one has difficulty getting to sleep or staying asleep. Often there will be early morning awakening and inability to return to sleep. Most will describe the feeling of being tired and wanting to go to sleep, but they toss and turn, taking hours to finally fall asleep.

3. Loss of Energy or Fatigue If one awakens refreshed but becomes more tired toward the middle or end of the day, there is a strong possibility that something other than depression is the problem. The depressed person feels tired or sluggish from the onset of the day, with difficulty getting out of bed and getting started. He will take, or at least want to take, naps during the day. Often there will be a shift of the sleep pattern, going to bed later (because he knows he will take a long time to fall asleep anyway) and arising later in the day when possible.

Probably one-third of all the patients I have diagnosed and treated for depression have initially complained of feeling tired, and thought they were anemic or had mononucleosis, or some other similar illness.

Many people are desperately groping for answers by using vitamins, dieting or improving nutrition, exercise, taking positive thinking classes, etc., all of which are good things in improving health, but will not cure depression. They will be an aid to recovery once the proper treatment is instituted, but alone will bring only disappointment and frustration, if true chemical depression exists.

4. Difficulty performing tasks or having an "overwhelmed" feeling This is a feeling difficult to describe, but those who are depressed will quickly recognize it and know exactly what I am talking about. I'm talking about looking at a load of laundry and getting a sick overwhelming feeling that it is just "too much." An ordinarily simple task becomes a huge obstacle, and the person literally has to force himself to accomplish it.

The employee on the job will have to force himself to make a phone call, or answer a letter, or any of a hundred simple tasks he is used to doing. Everything requires extra effort and often the depressed person feels like he is sinking in a hole with no bottom. Along with this, he experiences slowed movements, so everything takes longer. Ambition and drive seem to be lacking. Work productivity is often affected, and this added pressure is threatening.

5. Loss of interest or pleasure Normal interest in sex is decreased. In fact, it will often disappear altogether. This causes frustration for the spouse and guilt for the depressed person.

It is difficult to enjoy other things too. There is little enthusiasm, even for things that the person used to look forward to doing. Present also, may be lack of interest in interacting with other people, even to the point of avoiding others. There seems to be no pleasure in any activity. Often the pleasure and interest in eating diminishes. People drop out of bowling leagues, weekly get-togethers, or night classes. One doesn't have to be totally withdrawn from society or have complete melancholy, although this can happen in severe cases. It is just that things don't seem fun anymore.

6. Change in appetite and weight A loss of appetite with weight loss is more common, but depression may cause an increase in appetite with weight gain. If the depressed person has a significant amount of anxiety, he may eat more and gain weight. More commonly, the depressed person has lost interest in many things, including eating. Constipation, diarrhea or other digestive symptoms may appear.

7. Lowered self-esteem The depressed person will have feelings of worthlessness with a low self-esteem. He may feel sinful, guilty and unwanted, even though he knows he has no reason to feel that way. He blames himself for what is happening, and feelings of despair are overwhelming when he cannot push himself to improve his situation. He may feel like a burden to others. A truly depressed person may not feel like living at all.

8. Reduced ability to concentrate Depression causes slowed mentation, or thought processes. It makes thinking less clear and calculations slower. It goes along with feeling tired, and the sluggish behavior of the depressed. It is hard to overcome that "who cares" attitude. In this debilitated state, it is harder to organize thoughts, make decisions, to study or to complete projects. This is usually quite subtle, not generally causing alarm, unless accompanied by other of the listed characteristics.

9. Thoughts of suicide This is one symptom that varies in proportion to the severity of depression. Those with mild to moderate depression, will often feel like life is just not worth living, and that they want to give up, but they don't really have specific thoughts about taking their lives. When depression becomes more severe, people often feel they would actually rather be dead than live in this hopeless state. They begin thinking about death. They start to think of ways to kill themselves and may or may not voice their intentions.

Let me take a moment to clear up a few misconceptions about suicide. It is wrong to think that if a person threatens suicide he won't really do it. Any person voicing this concern should be taken seriously and immediate help should be obtained. If he talks about it, one can be sure he has thought about it many times before.

As mentioned, many people with depression will feel like giving up, or that life is just not worth living. There is a real risk of suicide in those depressed people who feel like their future is hopeless or that there is no way out. Depression can lead to suicide when reassurance from their physician or family and friends does not sink in, or is met with suspicion. Sometimes no professional help is sought.

Key phrases should alert one to the high possibility of suicide and immediate help should be obtained. Such key phrases include, "Everyone would be better off if I were dead." "I would rather be dead than continue on this way." "Just leave me alone or I'll end it all."

One should not be afraid to ask the depressed person if suicide has been considered. It is usually a relief for someone contemplating suicide to be able to talk about it.

There are certain groups of people who are at higher risk of suicide than others. These people should be watched more closely and help sought at any sign of suicide thoughts. These high risk groups include:

(a) Alcoholics or drug dependent persons, especially if they have sustained recent added stress.

(b) Elderly people, especially those taking many medications, or those with chronic diseases, and who are not expected to recover.

(c) Those who are depressed, especially if the depression is severe.

(d) Those who frequently talk about suicide, or those that have attempted suicide before.

(e) Those with increased stress in their lives: stresses such as financial difficulty, recent divorce or separation and loss of a loved one.

(f) Teenagers who are at highest risk, include those involved with alcohol and/or drugs, those with declining academic achievement, and those involved in delinquent behavior. Also at higher risk for suicide are the loners and those whose performance is far below the expectations placed on them by their families.

All talk of suicide and gestures need to be taken seriously. Contact your local hotline or physician for assistance in dealing with a suicidal friend or relative.

10. Physical complaints Persons with depression may have a variety of physical complaints. The most common are headache, backache, and gastrointestinal disturbances (stomachaches, diarrhea, or constipation). These symptoms alone would not identify depression, but they may accompany other of the symptoms. It may seem strange to think of depression causing real physical symptoms, but it can do just that. It may be related to improper nerve transmissions or to an altered level of a hormone called Cortisol. Regardless of the exact mechanism of action, the pain and disturbances are real and not imagined. Often complaints like diarrhea or a rash will disappear once treatment has been instituted.

More unusual physical or "somatic" symptoms may include light headedness, burning tongue pain, breast pain, leg, arm, or chest pain. Anytime a person repeatedly seeks medical help for many different unrelated physical ailments, the physician should always be alert to consider depression as the cause.

The person who is moody and has four or more of the above symptoms for longer than two weeks has depression. But why does he or she, or you, have it when someone else does not? What is it that causes depression?

Factors Affecting Depression

In the past, depression was described as endogenous, from within, or exogenous, from external causes. It was considered exogenous if there was an apparent problem or situation that started the depression. People who have this type of depression have a physiologic response to stress. Any stress can be a triggering cause of depression. It may be a major life stress, such as divorce, loss of a loved one, or losing a job. It may be something less severe, but still very stressful, such as moving, financial problems, job demands, family difficulties, childbearing, or any number of other stress events.

Many studies have been done in an attempt to demonstrate that depression is related to stress. One study[11] examined 134 housewives whose average age was forty-four. It was found that the greater the marital conflict over expectations of the female role in the family, the greater the degree of her dissatisfaction in housework. They went further to show that the greater the dissatisfaction in doing housework, the greater the chance for depression.

Another study[12] examined 1,091 people, both male and female. This study showed that there was a direct relationship between depression and external factors. Those who were exposed to higher stress situations

[11] *Sex Roles,* IX (November 1983), 1115-1125.

[12] *Research in Community and Mental Health,* III (1983) 113-139.

were more likely to become depressed. These variables included work dissatisfaction, prior illness, marital and parental status.

One journal article,[13] after studying 464 men and 647 women, concluded that absence of marriage and absence of employment were both associated with increased incidence of depression for both men and women. It also concluded that women at home, especially those with young children, were likely to have higher stress, and were definitely more likely to suffer from depression than other women.

There has been debate about whether the prevalence of depression is greater in women than in men. Most studies conclude that it is probably equal among both sexes, but women are more likely to seek help, therefore more are reported in the available data. Many researchers propose that it is more common in younger women, ages 20 to 40, but men, 55 to 60 have a higher frequency of depression. Perhaps this may be explained by the 20 to 40 year-old group of women being housewives and rearing children.

Among women, the highest rates of depression are found among the young, the poor, the mothers of small children, and those who are single heads of households. These women are faced with rearing families alone, while receiving very little emotional support. Many of these also have additional financial and social problems.

The 55 to 60 year-old group of men are faced with the reality of their limitiations. Boredom and loss of self-esteem associated with retirement may compound the other conditions of the elderly, such as poor health, waning strength, and the deaths of friends.

Some experts argue that environmental factors do not play a major role in depression. However, it is more than coincidence that nearly half of all depres-

[13] *Journal of Health and Social Behavior,* XXIX (December 1983), 300-312.

sion follows a major stress or life crisis. In examining environmental factors, logic would allow that a major stress could trigger a chemical imbalance, which is indicated from studies of stress upon body functions. Thus, if the body systems are not able to correct the imbalance, its continuance would initiate depression.

We know that millions of people have suffered depression as a reaction to stress. But many have had stresses to the same degree and have not become chemically depressed over a long period of time. In addition, many people have had severe depression with no precipitating stressful events, and no underlying reason that could be identified. In these cases, everything seemed to be going well. Those studied had a great family life, no financial problems, no stressful event . . . yet they became depressed and exhibited the exact same symptoms as those who did experience upsetting events. This type of depression was called endogenous depression — or that with no apparent cause. In my practice I have seen more "endogenous depression" with no apparent cause than I have "exogenous depression," or those with a reaction to stress. Probably about sixty percent of my cases have been endogenous Reports from the literature seem to support this as generally true.[14] But I do not like to classify my patients into endogenous or exogenous categories because, regardless of the type, the symptoms are the same, the treatment is the same, and the response to therapy is the same.

Even the Diagnostic and Statistical Manual of Mental Disorders (DSM-III) does not classify them as such anymore. They group these cases into one category and call the problem "unipolar depression." It can, however, be helpful to recognize an underlying problem if the depression is being treated and the problem is still present. This is when counseling and psychotherapy can be of benefit. Still the depressed

[14] Watts, p. 73.

person cannot effectively deal with this, or any problem, until the depression is treated.

As stated above, DSM-III calls what we have discussed, "unipolar depression" and this includes anyone who has symptom number one, plus any four other symptoms previously discussed. Unipolar means that these symptoms persist and these people stay at this low level (one plane).

Another, more rare form of depression, is called "bipolar depression." Often referred to as Manic Depressive Disorder, the symptoms of bipolar depression involve cycles of mania and depression. When in the depressive phase of the disorder, an individual may suffer from any or all of the symptoms associated with the unipolar depressive disorder.

Elated mood, insomnia, increased talking, social, sexual and physical activity are typical during the manic phase. The patient may possess abundant energy and have grandiose and unrealistic notions. The manic patient may feel capable of any undertaking, and tends to overlook any painful or harmful consequences of his behavior. In extreme cases, the manic depressive may experience thought disorders: jumping from one idea to another with no apparent connection, sometimes to the point of delusions and hallucinations.

The manic phase of a bipolar disorder can be just as disruptive as the depressive part of depression. I recently had a husband literally force his wife into my office because he could not sleep, due to her vacuuming, doing laundry, exercising, etc., night and day. She had slept a total of only four hours in the previous five days and nights. She was suffering from a manic phase of bipolar depression.

Causes of Depression

As previously mentioned, some people have depression as a result of stress, while others have no apparent reason. Even in those with reactive or exogenous depression, what made one person develop depression when another person with the same or worse stress did not? Two people with similar backgrounds and similar circumstances may go through life well enough, when, let us say at age thirty, the same event disrupts both lives, such as the loss of a spouse through death. They will both be naturally depressed as they go through the grief process, but one person has the ability to come back out of the depression, whereas the other will not. His depression continues for weeks, months or years. The same thing could happen after having a stressful family situation, or after having a child. What is it that allows one person to bounce back and handle these situations, and another to become disabled by depression? What is it that allows a person to handle thirty years of stress and then suddenly lose his ability to cope?

Most researchers agree that this difference is caused by a chemical imbalance in the body. This imbalance can surface with no precipitating factors, or it can be aggravated or triggered by factors such as those we mentioned previously.

There is probably a genetic or inherited factor to consider also. Although the exact mechanism by which depressive disorders are transmitted from one generation to another are not yet known, there is growing evidence that a genetic factor is involved, like we see in some other physical illnesses, such as heart disease or cancer.

Studies have shown that if one identical twin suffers from depression, there is a seventy percent likelihood that the other twin will also be affected.

Perhaps even more suggestive of a genetic factor are studies of adopted individuals carried out in New York and Brussels.[15] These researchers identified

[15] Public Health Services D.H.H.S. Publication No. (A.D.M.) 82-1081 (U.S. Department of Human Services, 1981), p. 3.

adoptees having depression. They then examined the rate of depression among their adoptive parents compared to their biological or natural parents. They found a higher incidence among the adoptees and their natural parents than with those who had adopted and reared them.

A similar study was done in Denmark, which included first and second degree relatives of both natural and adopting families, and found that the rate of occurrence of depression was three times greater among the natural relatives. Because of the higher incidence of depression in natural families, it gives some evidence to the fact that depression may involve a genetic factor. What this means to you and me is that if a person is a member of a family which has or has had members with depression, they are at higher risk of a depressive episode in their lifetime, than someone who has no family history of depression.

In the 1950's physicians first noticed that there were medications that caused mood swings. Some high blood pressure medications caused depression. Some medications used to treat tuberculosis caused people to feel "high" or euphoric. It was discovered that some hyperactive children could be better controlled with a certain medication. All these observations led clinicians to think that perhaps mood disorders could be due to a biochemical disturbance — and perhaps could be corrected with proper medication.

Further evidence of depression being linked to a chemical imbalance is found in postpartum baby blues, Premenstrual Syndrome (PMS), and menopausal depression. We know of many physiological changes brought about by different hormone levels, by observing side effects of birth control pills and increased or decreased estrogen or progesterone levels. An improper balance of certain chemicals or hormones has been suspected of causing depression for a long time, but only in the past few years have giant strides been made in finding the cause and treatment of depression.

The Chemical Imbalance

Animal brain tissues have been studied, and a group of chemical compounds called biogenic animes have been shown to regulate mood. The two most important biogenic amines are called serotonin and norepinephrine. They are concentrated in areas of the brain which also control such drives as hunger, sex, and thirst. Serotonin is associated with drowsiness and may be responsible for the fatigue seen in depression. Norepinephrine is released by nerve cells in the brain, and it appears to be related to arousal and alertness.

Serotonin and norepinephrine are among the many chemical compounds known as neurotransmitters. Neurotransmitters are chemical messengers that transmit electrochemical signals from one nerve cell to another in the brain. These neurotransmitters set in motion the complex chemical interactions that control our behavior, feelings and thoughts. It is similar to an electric wire going through a circuit to a light bulb. If you decrease the amount of voltage, or put a resister through the circuit, the light bulb becomes dim. Figure 1 illustrates how the chemical neurotransmitter works.

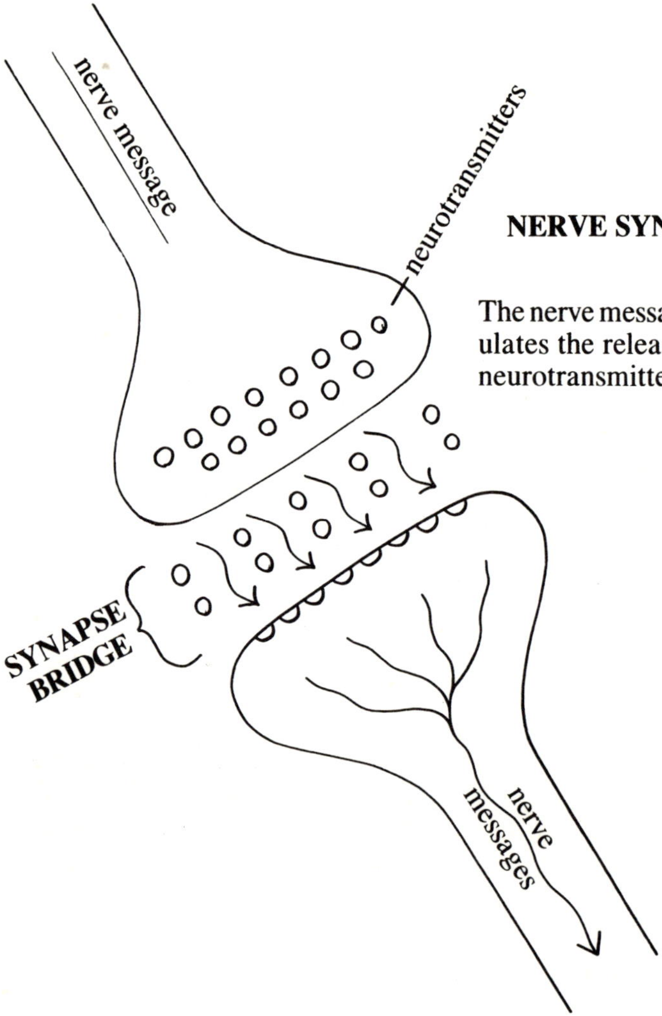

NERVE SYNAPSE

The nerve message stimulates the release of the neurotransmitters.

Figure 1

When the electrochemical message comes down the nerve and reaches the synapse bridge, the neurotransmitters are released, and they go across this nerve bridge carrying the message which stimulates the next nerve. After the neurotransmitters have crossed that bridge to carry the message, some of them go back to await the next transmission (sort of like a ferry taking cars across a river). However, some of them are taken back up by the body system, leaving a deficiency in transmitters. The next message to be delivered may not be carried properly because of a lack of neurotransmitters. When messages are not transmitted properly or adequately, problems arise in the body which manifest themselves as various symptoms.

When we understand the wide variety of functions that the nerve centers control, it is not hard to understand how one medical illness, namely depression, can be responsible for such a variety of symptoms. It can be responsible not only for mood changes, but everything from weight loss or gain to backache or stomach irritation.

We now have the capability to measure with a blood test, the amount of neurotransmitters of a person. If we measure the norepinephrine or serotonin blood levels of a depressed patient, we find that they are decreased.

Thus, we see that there are many theories to explain the cause of depression. Basically most of the theories relate to a chemical imbalance in the body. Perhaps an underlying genetic trait exists in some people, and a stressful situation tilts the delicate chemical balance. Maybe the same genetic predisposition to having a low level of neurotransmitters needs no stress to cause depression in others. No one is absolutely certain what causes depression, but we now understand a great deal about what is happening inside the body during depression. Whatever the cause, we can be grateful that there is an effective treatment, once it has been diagnosed.

How Depression Is Diagnosed

With the advent of new knowledge and interest in depression, several diagnostic tests have been developed to help diagnose depression. Many are experimental or are still in research stages. Others are easy to perform but the results aren't specific enough to make the diagnosis. Here I will briefly discuss some of the more widely available lab studies that can be performed.

As already mentioned, depression is associated with a decreased level of norepinephrine and seratonin, or as they are called, catecholamines (chemicals that help transmit nerve impulses). The level of these chemicals can be measured in the blood, and if a person has depression, the level of either one or both will be low.

When neurotransmitters are not readily available due to the chemical deficiencies, proper messages are not carried across from nerve to nerve, and certain physiological changes are manifested. Such symptoms may include muscle tension, heart and respiration rate changes. In addition, body cells may retain more salt than usual and bring about an imbalance in the electrical charges within the nervous system. The test measuring catecholamines may have a great deal of potential in helping the physician treat depression by knowing which chemical needs replacement. However, it is currently performed at a limited number of places, and is too expensive to be productive for mass screening.

There are other chemical levels which change when a person is depressed, that can be measured by laboratory testing. One of these is cortisol, which is a steroid produced by the adrenal gland. It is an essential hormone that provides resistance to a variety of stresses like cold, or response to anger and fear. It also maintains the activity of numerous enzyme systems and is probably related to sleep disturbance, body aches, pains, and tiredness experienced by those who are depressed. Depressed people have too much cortisol produced by their adrenal gland. Cortisol levels may be determined by a blood test, but the results cannot alone prove or disprove depression.

Another laboratory test that may prove helpful in clinical practice is the Dexamethasone Suppression Test (DST). While it is not yet a part of regular medical practice in diagnosing depression, it is being used by many physicians and hospitals and may become more widely utilized. This test is currently receiving much attention in the media. But because there is a tendency to exaggerate its usefulness or misunderstand what this test is about, let's review how it works and what it can accomplish.

Many people with serious depression produce an excess amount of cortisol as mentioned above. When normal people are given another chemical hormone called dexamethasone, the regulating system of the body gets the message that there is enough hormone in the bloodstream and production of cortisol is suppressed, usually for about a day. However, in the depressed person the cortisol production is suppressed only briefly, then climbs high again in less than a day. So after taking dexamethasone at midnight, the 8:00 a.m. test for cortisol is not low as it should be. If this level is too high, it is likely that the person tested has depression. However, there are many other medical problems that can cause this same result. Therefore, the DST alone does not determine depression. It can, however, be an aid in the diagnostic process.

There are many other tests being studied in research laboratories around the world. They measure factors in blood, urine, or brain waves. Most are not specific enough to be used alone in the diagnosis of depression.

Perhaps, one day, research will make available a single, diagnostic test like we have for diabetes for instance. But does this mean we cannot make the diagnosis of depression? Absolutely not. In the majority of cases, the diagnosis can be made from the symptoms present. Your physician can determine if special tests are needed to rule out a disorder that can have similar symptoms. Many times, one with little medical knowledge can get a good idea whether or not someone is depressed by reviewing the symptoms listed in chapter two. If four or more symptoms are present and have been affecting the person's normal lifestyle for longer than two weeks, then the diagnosis is most likely depression. It should, however, be ultimately diagnosed, or at least confirmed by a physician who can also give an adequate physical examination to rule out disorders that may be similar to the symptoms of depression.

Again let me take a moment to re-emphasize the point that true depression does not mean that one is "crazy" or has a problem "in their head." It is an actual, proven imbalance of chemicals. Now with the understanding that it is a variety of symptoms all caused by a decrease in either serotonin or norepinephrine, or both, one should also realize that exercise, change in attitude, or other "home remedies" are not going to change a person who is actually suffering from a disease caused by a chemical imbalance until that balance is restored.

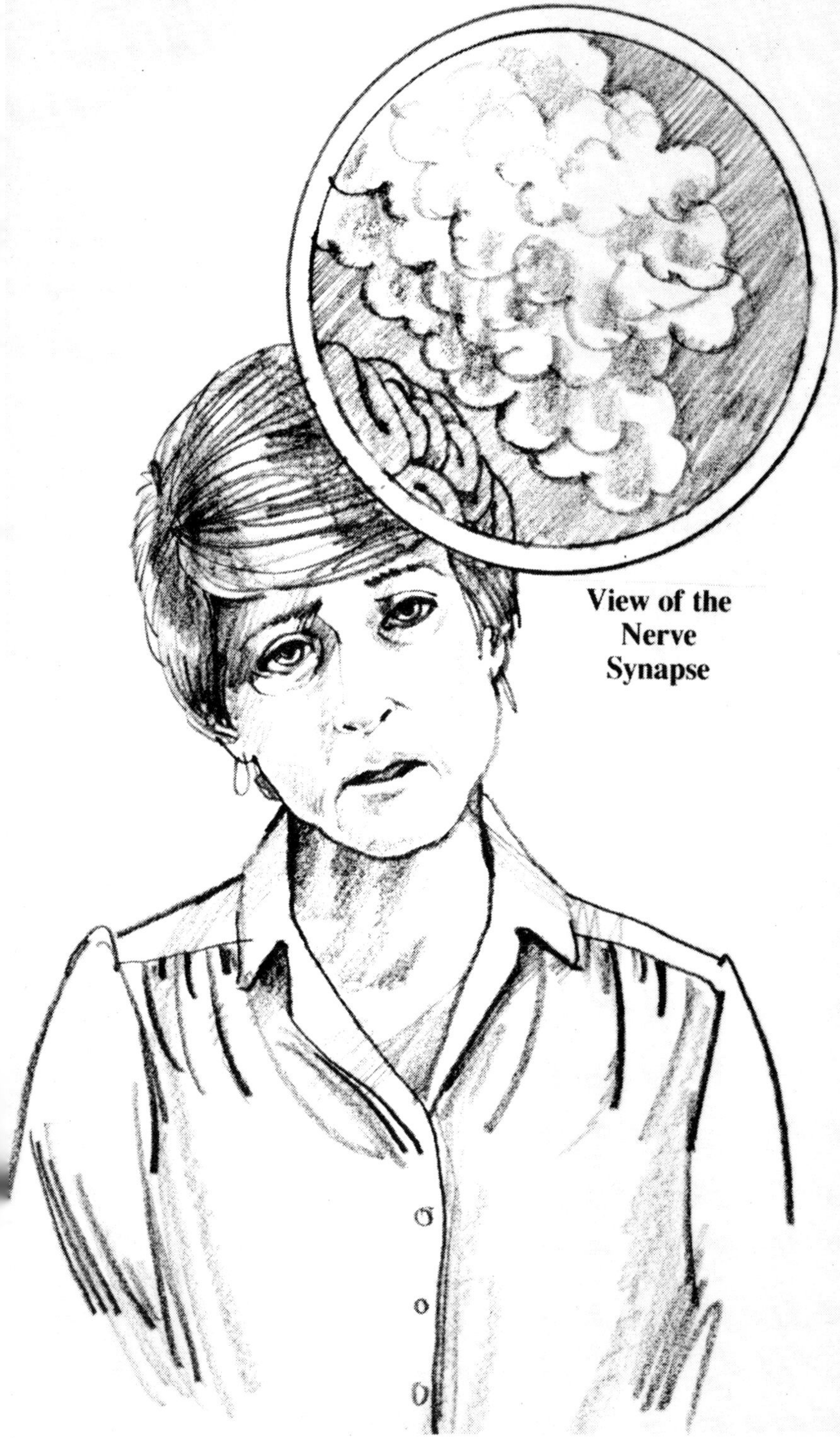
View of the Nerve Synapse

CHAPTER THREE

And The Good News Is . . .

When someone has high blood pressure or hypertension, he is treated with a medicine called antihypertensives because hypertension is a physical medical illness that could potentially cause harm. When someone has arthritis he is treated with anti-inflammatory drugs. If someone has an infection he is treated with antibiotics because an infection is a medical illness. Depression is a medical illness, too, and it is treated with antidepressants.

While people with hypertension and arthritis would definitely rather be without it, they don't go around feeling guilty about it. People with depression, on the other hand, not only suffer intensely with their symptoms, they feel guilty about it. In my opinion, severe depression is the most devastating illness known to man, and its agony is made worse by feelings of guilt.

Depressed patients and their families must realize that depression is a disease of physical and biochemical character, and their feelings of guilt have no justification.

We discussed earlier that depression can be a term used for temporary melancholy or transient blues, but true chemical depression is a chemical imbalance. How we treat depression depends on which type it is.

Take, for example, diabetes. This disease occurs when blood sugar level required for energy is too high in the blood stream because it can't get across the cell membrane to be broken down. There are two types of diabetes: one requires insulin and the other does not. Non-insulin dependent diabetes is referred to as hyperglycemia and can often be treated with weight loss, careful diet and exercise. But if one has insulin dependent diabetes, there is a lack of insulin (a chemical in the body which carries sugar across the cell membrane). In this case, diet, weight loss and exercise do no good, and the diabetic is required to use insulin injections. Without insulin the diabetic would have problems so severe he would die.

Depression is much the same. If we speak of the blues, then many treatment options are available. Counselors or religious leaders can often provide support and assist in working through problems that are causing the transient depression. Getting involved in different activities, service to others, developing a positive attitude, exercise, and a good diet are all things that will improve a temporary feeling of depression.

But in cases of true chemical depression, these things will not work. People who are depressed can hardly pull themselves out of bed, or get through a day of work, let alone get involved in new activities or exercise. In fact, attempting to treat chemical depression by these methods often leads to intense frustration because the individual does not feel better, which in turn, results in lowered self-esteem and deepens the depression.

There have been studies done to evaluate the effects of exercise, such as aerobics and running as a treatment for chemical depression. These studies revealed little support for improvement of any symptom of depression or anxiety, and concluded that exercise as antidepressant treatment was unwarranted.[16]

[16] *Journal of Sports Psychology*, V(1983), 288-301.

Antidepressant Medications Work

When depression is chemical, its treatment must also be chemical. Most of the antidepressant drugs used now, come from a family of medicines called tricyclic antidepressants. It is very important to understand what antidepressants are, and perhaps equally as important to understand what they are not.

Tricyclic antidepressants are not tranquilizers or sleeping pills. They are not uppers or downers, nor are they stimulants. They are not addicting, and they are not harmful to the body. They are medications that help replace the natural chemicals that have reached low levels in the body — chemicals that are essential to normal well-being.

Neurotransmitter chemicals carry messages across the nerve synaptic bridge. After these neurotransmitters have delivered the message to the next nerve ending, some of them return back to the first nerve to await the next nerve impulse and some of these chemicals are taken up by the body system, making them less available in the synaptic bridge to carry the next message. Tricyclic drugs decrease the uptake of these chemicals by the body system, allowing more norepinephrine and seratonin to be available for use. Thus it increases the level of these vital neurotransmitters by blocking their uptake or absorption by the body. More chemicals are then available to carry on their essential role and the symptoms start to disappear.

One can expect the medicine to alleviate such symptoms as decreased capacity to feel pleasure, irritability, low self-esteem, loss of social and sexual interest, psychomotor retardation (having to force oneself to do things), decreased ability to concentrate, feelings of being overwhelmed and hopelessness. More than just a little change may be expected. In most cases there is complete resolution of these symptoms.

Let me pause here to tell you a few facts about tricyclic medication. First, they do have some side effects, though most are just temporary. Many tricyclics cause the patient to be more tired or sleepy during the first few days. This is temporary.

These medications affect all people differently. I gave one tricyclic to a young lady. She took the pills at bedtime and she didn't awaken till three o'clock the next afternoon. I have given the same medicine to other people who usually can't sleep at night, and it didn't even make them drowsy. Everyone will react differently. The side effect of drowsiness wears off relatively quickly. The first day of medication, drowsiness is the most predominant side effect, but each day it lessens, until it is gone. Usually the first three or four days are the worst.

If a person has difficulty falling asleep or staying asleep, the physician may purposely choose a tricyclic that has a side effect of drowsiness, and instruct the patient to take a larger dosage at bedtime. Some types should be taken two to three hours before bedtime because it will take that long to take effect. Others seem to start causing drowsiness within half an hour. Only a physician can determine the correct times the medication can be taken and the correct dosage for each individual patient.

Another side effect is dryness of the mouth, which may make the tongue feel big. It may also cause increased thirst. This side effect will last the longest and may not go away. This can be partially alleviated by drinking more water and chewing gum. It is a very small price to pay for the relief of the other depressive symptoms. Other side effects may or may not appear. They can include such things as constipation, difficulty starting urination, blurred vision, light-headedness, weight gain and flushing. These are not common, and if they are present, they are usually temporary. If they are a problem, they should be reported to the physician who started treatment.

The next point that needs to be made is that tricyclics usually take about two weeks to begin working. That means for the first one to two weeks, the patient may have to cope with the negative effects and yet not experience the good effects. Some may start experiencing the good effects after only three or four days, and some may take three or four weeks. I have found the average person is over the side effects and has begun to experience a change of symptoms after ten to fourteen days of treatment. The physician may choose to evaluate the patient at this time.

Let me also explain that not everyone will experience results with every tricyclic medication. There are many types of tricyclics; each of them elevate to different degrees, either norepinephrine and/or seratonin. In my experience, I have found that approximately one of every six people will not respond to the first tricyclic chosen and must be switched to another. Most physicians will evaluate the patient at two to four weeks, at which point, an improvement of symptoms is usually evident. If the improvement isn't as expected, the physician may choose to increase the dosage or change to a different tricyclic.

Because each tricyclic affects norepinephrine or seratonin to a different degree, each has a somewhat different side effect profile. Because different anti-depressants have different side effects, the best one for the individual needs to be chosen by the physician. For those people who do not respond to one, another one may work well. There is continued research and a continuing line of new drugs being developed.

Time Factors In Treatment

How long does one stay on antidepressents? Without antidepressant therapy, episodes of clinical depression last from two months to several years, with an average of five to six months. One-third of the patients recover within a year. An estimated one out of four untreated episodes last more than two years.[17]

When the time comes to stop antidepressants, the doctor will stress the importance of tapering down the dosage and not stopping abruptly. Therefore, under the doctor's supervision, the patient decreases the dosage very slowly. **I cannot overstate this point.**

After decreasing the dosage a small amount, the physician will probably recommend staying at the dosage for a minimum of two weeks. If, at the end of that time the patient feels as well as at the beginning of the two week period, then the dosage may be decreased again and so on, according to the doctor's prescription. If, however, the patient feels the symptoms of depression recurring, he should immediately check with the physician.

Clinical experience and research seems to indicate that although most patients do recover from episodes of major depression, a significant number do not, and begin a chronic course of depressive illness. The rate of the chronic or long-lasting depression is reported in the medical literature from between one percent to twenty-eight percent. But one study from 1984 examined ninety-seven patients who met the criteria for depression, and followed them for two years.[18] This study showed that 64% had recovered by six months, 74% at one year, and 79% at the two year follow-up period. After examining the 21% who had not recovered after two years, one thing was found in common; not age, not severity of depression, not sex, or social status — but the length of time they had been depressed. It showed that the longer a patient had

[17] Heinz E. Lehmann M.D., "Clinical Evaluation and Natural Course of Depression," *Journal of Clinical Psychiatry,* IVL (May 1983), 5.

[18] Moutra B. Keller M.D., et al., "Long Term Episodes of Major Depression," *Journal of the American Medical Association,* CCLII No. 6, (August 10, 1984), 788-792.

been ill, the greater the likelihood of remaining chronically ill for a longer period of time. It also indicated that about one-fifth of patients who receive treatment at university medical centers for episodes of depression will not recover for at least two years after they seek treatment. Some may not recover at all. Most studies show a higher rate of success with medication, but this research does suggest that treatment should begin as soon as possible after the onset of symptoms to improve the chances of recovery.

Other Considerations of Treatment

Because nearly everyone responds to one of the tricyclic antidepressants, only brief mention will be made of other forms of treatment. When tricyclics fail, there is a drug class known as monoamine oxidase inhibitors (MAO inhibitors) that may be tried. This class of drugs is actually older than tricyclics but have potentially more harmful effects on the body and are now used only if tricyclics fail. The MAO inhibitors are particularly useful in patients who eat or sleep excessively.

Lithium is effective against bipolar depression in which the lows of depression alternate with the highs of mania when one is extremely hyper-anxious. It reduces the frequency and severity of the manic-depressive cycles. Lithium controls the mania ·like insulin does diabetes. Here again, this drug requires closer supervision than does the tricyclics because of delicate balance of blood levels that could cause other harmful side effects.

Electro-convulsive therapy (ECT) now is used less frequently with the availability of the tricyclic anti-depressants. Nonetheless, ECT remains an effective method of treatment for those few people who have severe depression, and who do not respond to any other treatment. Current ECT practices are designed to be effective, safe and painless. Before treatment, the patient is put to sleep and a muscle relaxant is given. In trained hands, ECT is safe and effective for those few people who need it.

Treatment is the First Step

Now that you have an understanding of what tricyclic antidepressants can do, let me emphasize some of their limitations. When a proper dosage is reached and maximum benefit from the medicine obtained, one can expect resolution of the symptoms of depression. Irritability, sleep and appetite disturbances will be corrected, self-esteem and ability to think and concentrate will improve and the sex drive will return. Somatic, or physical, complaints like headache, backache, stomachache, etc. will disappear only if they are related to depression. Energy and ambition will return to normal.

It is necessary to note of course, that medication will not balance the checkbook, return a deceased loved one, make a teenager suddenly obedient, or solve any other problem not related to symptoms of depression. What it does do, is allow people to cope with these problems. They can face the problems, if any, and more reasonably find solutions and have the drive to carry out actions and decisions, when a balanced body chemistry is restored.

If the depression is endogenous (no apparent causing factor from outer circumstances), tricyclic antidepressants are usually all that is needed. The response to medication is good and the relief of symptoms dramatic. If depression is a result of stress or other underlying problem (exogenous or reactive depression) antidepressant medication is still required.

In addition to medication, counseling is often beneficial and sometimes essential for successful treatment.

For those people with depression, medical treatment is definitely good news since the advent of tricyclic antidepressants. But the first step in treatment is recognizing the problem and gaining an understanding of the disease process we call depression. It is important to realize that it is a real and physical condition that attacks about one of every five people at sometime in their lives.

Part of treatment is stopping the fuel of guilt from feeding the fire of depression. There is no need to feel guilty, and one must understand that the tired lack of ambition, the decreased mental sharpness, and increased feelings of hopelessness are all part of depression. The spouse needs to be understanding and realize that many of the things said by the affected person are not indications of true feelings. Often just understanding the disease and knowing that these symptoms are normal, make the ability to cope much easier for both the depressed individual, and for their families and friends.

Along with understanding depression goes the need to understand limitations. Whether or not depression is the result of a stressful event, once depression is manifest, stress always makes it worse. Added responsibilities should not be undertaken, and life should be kept as simple as possible. If someone had broken a leg, people would not expect him to continue his bowling league or jogging until it healed. The same logic should be used by the depressed; they should take it easy and not add any extra stress.

People who have had a bad day and feel they just can't cope should, if possible, forget the task that is causing the stresss and think of something that sounds more appealing. For example, if someone had planned to clean out the garage, but can't force himself to do it, then he should choose something else to do, like working on an enjoyable project. If one is at work and can't face an inventory, or can't finish a report — and it doesn't have to be done that day — then to hold a planning meeting or to do something else productive and appealing, is a good idea.

If one is feeling down without having true chemical depression, then eliminating stress, simplifying life, improving exercise and diet, and understanding the symptoms, is sufficient for treatment. After reading the symptoms of chemical depression however, and if you feel you may have it, then using the above steps may help as a beginning.

If they do not help, or if the symptoms persist — whether or not there is an apparent reason — then help from a physician should be sought. The doctor should be told all the symptoms that have led the patient to believe he has chemical depression. I recommend not waiting longer than two weeks to begin the self-help measures. If they fail to produce a dramatic reduction in symptoms after two weeks, or after the total of four weeks and the symptoms are still bad enough to interfere with normal life, then medical help is necessary. It has been shown that the earlier depression is treated, the better the chance for total and quick recovery.

We have come a long way in the understanding and treatment of depression. For those suffering from depression there is a light at the end of a very long, very dark, tunnel. Proper treatment saves marriages, eliminates hopeless frustrations, and saves lives. That's good news!

CHAPTER FOUR
Depression and PMS

Depression, in and of itself, is a frequent malady that affects millions of individuals. Depression also plays a major role in Pre-Menstrual Syndrome (PMS).

Characteristics of PMS

There has been a lot of interest in PMS as of late. Like depression, PMS is not a new disease. It is just that it now has a name. Isn't it interesting that for as long as we can remember it was just "that time of the month"? Excuses were automatic and jokes were made. But it took someone giving it a name before we were willing to take it seriously, search for a cause, and attempt treatment. How many people, in reflection of their own childhood, can remember their mother's frequent crying episodes and their having a few days to a week each month of being anxious, "touchy," and "out of sorts"? This was accepted as normal, and few questions were asked. Now the time has come for questions to be asked and answers found. Unlike depression, PMS has received good coverage by the lay media, but has not come into its own in the medical field.

What exactly is PMS? It is a symptom or group of symptoms that appear in a cyclic manner, usually preceding the menstrual cycle. Typically, symptoms appear during the last week of the normal menstrual cycle (one week prior to menstruation), but they may begin shortly after ovulation at about mid-cycle. Usually the symptoms disappear after the first day or two of the new cycle, so for many women, the symptoms of PMS may last half the month.

One of the most common symptoms of PMS is depression. This may be identical to unipolar chemical depression, and is often more intense. The feelings of hostility, mood swings, resentment, guilt, paranoia, irritability, tiredness and lack of self-esteem accompany other symptoms of sleep disturbance, decreased sex and social interest, and difficulty performing tasks. Arguments are frequent; family ties are strained and frustrations are taken out on spouses and children. It is bad enough that the symptoms of PMS are present up to half of every month, thus upsetting nearly half of the woman's life, but another very important concept is that the woman does not completely recover in one day and go on like nothing happened — nor do those around her, who have been affected by the syndrome of behavior displayed. There is a carry-over of the sick part of the month to the well part. Even though her character may return to normal, there have usually been some hostilities expressed during the bad weeks to cause serious problems. Frequently, harsh words are spoken in fits of rage from frustration or in retaliation to others. It is hard for marriages to survive when half the month is spent in depression and the other half is spent trying to mend the scars. Then just as things start to mend, the cycle repeats itself. Children are often greatly affected by this erratic change of personality.

One day everything is fine, and the next day, an action ordinarily not noticed brings down the wrath of an irate mother. The same inability to control emotions and anger can rekindle problems with friends and in-laws. Often these hostile expressions are not easily retracted.

As we become more aware of the effects of PMS, people should recognize that often the woman with PMS is not able to help the way she behaves. Husbands need to discount the things their wives say in anger. Family, friends and in-laws need to recognize this problem and be more understanding and sympathetic towards the woman's needs. They must be made to understand PMS for what it is: a chemical change occurring in the female body that distorts her emotions and behavior.

PMS is a condition that affects from 30 to 60 percent of all women. It can affect any woman at any age. It can, surprisingly, occur after menopause or even after hysterectomy. Depression is not the only symptom of PMS. In fact, over a hundred different symptoms have been attributed to it. Remember, PMS is only a symptom or group of symptoms occurring a certain number of days during the month on a cyclic basis.

The symptoms may include, in addition to depression, breast tenderness and swelling, abdominal bloating, headache, fatigue, edema or body swelling, irritability, anxiety, acne, constipation, increased appetite and/or itching and rash. There may also be other symptoms, but these are the most common. No one experiences all of the symptoms, but any combination of these can be found. The duration and severity also varies greatly.

Theories Vary on the Causes of PMS

There are almost as many theories about what causes PMS as there are symptoms. Traditionally, vitamin B6 deficiency has been blamed as the cause. This has been given credence by the discovery that Vitamin B6 acts as a coenzyme or a helper in the final production of seratonin. (Seratonin is one of the neurotransmitters that is at a low level in depression.) However, a deficiency actually corrected by vitamin

B6 replacement and thus relieving the symptoms of PMS remains to be demonstrated.[19]

Another possible cause of PMS symptoms is related to the hormone called progesterone.[20] Some think that there are women who may have an "allergy" to progesterone. This has been suspected for more than fifty years. The hormone progesterone is important for both men and women, but is more widely recognized in women because it, with estrogen, is used in birth control pills. It is also the hormone responsible for the preparation of the uterus for the reception and development of the fertilized egg. It is logical to suspect female hormones as a cause because PMS is, by definition, a series of symptoms occuring around a woman's menstrual period.

There is evidence to support the theory of an allergic reaction to the progesterone itself. There have been women who consistently break out in a rash during their menstrual cycle. It has been demonstrated that blood drawn from a person during a PMS episode could reproduce all or some of the symptoms of PMS, including a rash, if infused at a later date in that person when she is symptom-free. Even though some suggest that a psychological cause could be responsible for PMS, the vast majority of information suggests that it is a real, physical problem. I think it would be very difficult to consistently have symptoms such as bloating, flushing, nausea or vomiting, allergic reactions, acne, breast swelling, etc., all without a physical cause!

Even though most feel there is a physical cause, we recognize that behavior modification can alter PMS in some women. There are many clinics set up across the country that specifically treat PMS with behavior

[19] G.E. Abraham and J.T. Hargrove, "Effect of Vitamin B6 on Premenstrual Symptomotogy," *(Abstract) Infertility,* III(1980), 155-165, 1980.

[20] K. Dalton, "The Premenstraul Syndrome and Progesterone Therapy," London: *Heine Medical Book,* 1977.

modification. Because some symptoms of PMS can be altered with behavior modification does not mean there is not still a physical underlying disorder. It simply means that some of the symptoms can be altered by psychologic means. This should not surprise anyone. There are many medical problems caused by, or made worse by, stress, including altered menstrual flow, headache, and abdominal pain, just to mention a few.

Some have suggested that PMS is caused by altered hormones from different organ systems. For example, there are many symptoms that PMS has in common with low blood sugar — hunger, sweating, shaking or nervousness, and fatigue — but no significant relationship has been established.

Available Treatments

We know PMS exists and are aware of its symptoms. As already mentioned, the symptoms of PMS may vary greatly, so it stands to reason that there are a variety of treatments available. The treatment really depends on which symptoms are present and the severity of symptoms. I'll briefly describe some of the treatment options.

1. Dietary treatment. For women suffering mild to moderate symptoms, diet modification is often the only treatment needed. The good thing about dietary treatment is that not only is it natural, but it helps with good health in general and can do no harm. Probably the biggest disadvantage is that the results are slower in alleviating the problem. It usually takes about two months to determine which diet is best and another two to three months to begin experiencing positive results.

Ideally, the woman should keep a diet diary, keeping track of everything she eats and drinks in a three-day period right before her menstrual cycle, and compare this to the days just after her menstrual cycle. It is often very easy to see the change in diet that takes place when the two are compared. Some women may have a craving for junk food and increase the amount of sugars consumed. Others may increase the amount of dairy products or caffeine taken in during that three days. Often just stopping the sweets or limiting dairy products and caffeine will be enough to stop anxiety or irritability, decrease swelling, etc., Once this is accomplished, there are other things in the overall diet that could be changed to reduce symptoms. A good, balanced diet of 15% protein, 25% fats and 60% carbohydrates is recommended. Proteins should be more vegetable than animal, fats should be mostly from vegetable oils, and the carbohydrates should be made up mostly of complex carbohydrates such as vegetables, cereals and grains. A high fiber diet is also suggested. Thirty grams of fiber a day is a good goal and can be reached by eating raw vegetables and changing to whole wheat products in breads and cereals. Fiber can also be added easily to one's diet by sprinkling a tablespoon of bran, which can be purchased a a grocery store, on cereal each morning.

A sensible multi-vitamin supplement would not hurt, and may help. In some cases, adding extra vitamin A or vitamin B_6 two weeks before the menstrual cycle begins has proven helpful. Specific foods to avoid would be alcohol and caffeine and one should try to limit refined sugars and dairy products.[21]

2. **Water pills** can be beneficial in the treatment of premenstrual fluid retention, but is not a medicine without risk. They have the potential of altering the electrolyte balance and is usually reserved for those who have fluid retention only a few days of the month. Often, reduction or elimination of salt from the diet will eliminate the problem of fluid retention.

[21] Reproduced with permission from *Patient Care* May 15, 1985 © 1985, Patient Care Communications Inc., Darien, Ct. All rights reserved.

3. Birth control pills can be useful for some women. Some studies demonstrate that those women already on birth control pills have PMS symptoms less frequently than those who are not on them. But some studies show that when those on birth control pills do get symptoms, they are more severe. So although it may prevent symptoms in some women, it is not, as a general rule, good for stopping the symptoms when they are already present. If birth control is going to be used, then using the birth control pill may decrease the chance of having PMS symptoms. However, if severe depression is experienced while on the pill, you may want to talk to your physician about discontinuing the pill.

4. Progesterone has been used by many with good results, especially those who have severe premenstrual anxiety and irritability. This is obviously a treatment initiated by the doctor for those people he feels it will most benefit.

5. Antidepressants. Women who have cyclic depression may have the diagnosis of either PMS or depression. It doesn't matter because the symptoms and the treatment are the same. If a woman meets the criteria for depression as mentioned in Chapter Two, and the symptoms are severe enough or duration long enough to adversely affect her lifestyle, then treatment is indicated. Again the treatment for depression, whether it lasts all month or just seven days prior to her period, is stll antidepressants. Remember, antidepressents take from seven days to three or four weeks to reach their maximum effect, and so for this reason, many times it is not recommended that patients take them only during those days before their periods. In many cases, better control is obtained if the antidepressant is taken all month long. Sometimes combination therapy is needed using antidepressants with one or more other treatment options.

There are other drugs used, at times to specifically decrease breast tenderness, to work on anxiety and others to help swelling, etc., The main point here is that PMS is just a catch-all term for women having problems close to their menstrual period, and there is no single therapy for everyone suffering from its symptoms. Every person needs to be evaluated individually and treated according to their symptoms. Even women with the same symptoms may, and often do, respond differently to the same medications.

6. PMS Clinics. There are many clinics set up across the country specifically designed for women with PMS. Like everything else in life, there are good and bad ones. Some of the clinics treat only with behavior modification, others with diet, others with medication only. Some include physician evaluation including physical exams, while others do not. Some have initial workshops, some have ongoing workshops, some have classes, while others have physician evaluations. In cost, they can range from less than $50 to more than $500. Some charge by the hour, others by the treatment, while others have a set fee for the entire course. How does one choose the right clinic?

First of all, a clinic may not be necessary at all. I would start by seeing the personal physician first. Most symptoms of PMS can be handled by a physician from his office. We discuss how to choose an appropriate physician later on in this chapter. If a clinic is needed, then often-times the doctor can recommend one that would best suit one's needs.

Several general guidelines should be followed: 1) The qualifications of the health professional providing care at the center must be known. 2) Find out what is done and what their curriculum is. 3) Get a detailed explanation of how they evaluate and treat their patients. 4) See if they use more than one treatment. If diet is their only therapy or progesterone their sole treatment, regardless of the evaluation, then many people will fail to respond, because not everyone responds to the same treatment. 5) Consider whether the cost seems appropriate for the care given. 6) Check to see if the clinic claims to "have **the** answer to PMS." If they claim this, remember: there is no **one** answer to PMS.

PMS Summary

PMS and depression are major medical problems. They affect the lives of hundreds of thousands of individuals. The time has come now for people to become educated on the symptoms and cause of depression. Needless suffering can be avoided by proper diagnosis and treatment. If you or someone you know has symptoms of depression or PMS, seek the help of a physician as soon as possible. How does one choose a physician if you do not have one? The answer to this question is in the summary on page 76.

Keep in mind that it is normal for people with PMS associated depression to act in ways we have described, and that there is effective treatment that will restore light at the end of the long tunnel.

CHAPTER FIVE

Adolescent Depression

Depression in adolescents is even more complex than the chemical depression described by adults. Although it too, is a real and physical problem, it is intermixed with complex emotions of a boy or girl trying to become a young man or young woman. No one knows for sure how prevalent depression is in adolescents. We do know that suicide and suicide attempts are often the result of a severe depression, and suicide is the third leading cause of death in people ages 15-24. Only accidents and homicides are more prevalent. Many so-called accidents are actually suicides.

A Variety of Behaviors Signal Teen Depression

Delinquency, drug and alcohol abuse, criminal acts, rebellion, school truancy, sexual promiscuity, and self-destructive acts are not always, but often, the result of depression. These desperate acts are often ways of striking back against the terrible loneliness, confusion and anxiety associated with depression.

Symptoms of depression among adolescents are essentially the same as for the adult, but are adapted and acted out on their level. For example, decreased ability to concentrate may manifest itself as poor school performance. This change in ability to perform at school may lead to shame and guilt, and may be reason for skipping class. Missing class puts him further behind in school, which intensifies feeling of lowered self-esteem and guilt. The teenager will often then resolve to do better, but the depressed, hopeless feeling of being overwhelmed will not allow for needed change. In a frustrated effort to supress terrible feelings, the depressed adolescent may turn to alcohol, drugs, self-destructive tendencies, rebellion, fits of rage, or even to suicide. Other symptoms are sleep disturbance with resultant lethargy during the day, loss of interest in almost everything, physical complaints, irritability, personal sloppiness, change in eating habits and withdrawal from social life.

Adolescents who are depressed feel terribly alone. They experience an intense emptiness. There already exists an emptiness to some lesser degree, in the average adolescent. This is a time when they are struggling for security, while at the same time, they are breaking away from the most secure position they have ever experienced — that of being fully taken care of by their parents. They are no longer the "little darling." They are expected to act like an adult, yet their position is uncertain. Their roles are mixed and confusing. They are "too old to act that way," yet "too young" to be doing something else. Sometimes it is difficult for them to figure out exactly what is expected of them. The fortunate teenagers have been given unconditional love and patient understanding by nurturing parents. However, many times frustrated parents criticize their teenager's dress, their music or their friends. This is a time when the adolescent is struggling for acceptance and respect among peers. During this delicate balance of insecurity and the need for acceptance, the added weight of depression tips the scale to a devastating feeling of emptiness.

Those are pretty hard feelings to deal with, and the adolescent will usually try to hide them. They will work extra hard to prove themselves as an athlete or to gain top honors in drama, band, or any area of interest, while trying to disguise the tremendous turmoil within. They exert so much energy covering up their feelings that often they don't have time to relax and have fun.

To the Parent and Teenager

Dr. Avi Kiev wrote a book about adolescent depression entitled, Riding Through the Downers. In it, he wrote a letter to a depressed adolescent. Here is a portion of what he wrote, reproduced with Dr. Kiev's permission.

> Those are pretty hard feelings to live with, and I'm not surprised that you've been trying to bury them by pretending they don't exist. It's clear you don't feel very good, but from what you say it seems as if you'r acting just the opposite. Bad as you feel inside, you do what's expected of you with a stiff smile; like somebody constantly on stage, you keep your true emotions hidden.
>
> On the surface your acting seems to be working. Most people don't recognize your inner turmoil, and so you're successfully avoiding a lot of questions, conflicts and complaints. But you're using an enormous amount of energy to do this, and that energy is being subtracted from other areas of your life. Because you're working so hard at your disguise, you don't have time for much else. No wonder you're just "not interested" any more in things that used to please you.
>
> I know a long-term depression can be a pretty awful thing, because its specific symptoms, both physical and psychological, seem to nourish your feelings of despair. You wake up too early in the morning after

sleeping fitfully the night before. You've lost interest in food. You have no energy. Your arms and legs feel heavy. You suffer from headaches. You have feelings of dread which paralyze you when you get up, then mysteriously disappear sometime in the afternoon. You worry about school, and because you worry you can't concentrate, and that makes you worry more.

You've felt this way for months, and you've begun to feel alienated and reluctant to assume responsibility or follow any routine. You have trouble expressing yourself or asserting your point of view. You feel unappreciated, unloved, even worthless. External pressures, which seem overwhelming, make you angry, yet you are convinced you shouldn't feel that way and that you are strange or sick because you do. You're afraid to get angry with people you feel are pressuring you because you might explode, go to pieces or clobber someone. As bad as you feel, you're most afraid of losing control and doing something that will make you feel more guilty.

To top it off, you feel trapped in a situation you cannot change that is making you feel helpless. You feel your depression will never end, that no one will ever understand you, and that it's useless to try to do anything about it.

You may feel your entire life—even your own body—is out of your control. You may get the feeling that you are standing outside of your body watching yourself go through the motions of being alive—as if you were strapped into a chair watching yourself on TV. This is a common occurrence in depression. It's what we call a 'defense mechanism': a way that your mind turns off feelings of intolerable frustration by convincing you that the whole thing is out of your hands. If you don't understand how such a mechanism works, you can be very frightened by it, since it leaves you feeling that nothing is real and that your mind is separate from your body. This explains the feeling of numbness you describe which has led you to want to cut yourself to see if you'd bleed. No wonder you say you are afraid of 'losing your mind.'

You say too that you can't relate to others any more; a thick, invisible glass wall seems to divide you from everybody you know, and gives you the feeling of being trapped inside your own body. Paradoxically, at the same time everybody seems to be pushing you to do this or do that, to be this way or that way; nobody leaves you enough elbow room to do what you want to do. And since you're not at all sure yourself what that is, you're an easy mark for unsolicited suggestions, advice and 'help.'

Worst of all, you're preoccupied with recurring morbid thoughts, in addition to an extreme sense of guilt about your apparent inability to act. The same images keep jamming your head, coming back over and over again, until all you want to do is get rid of them. You feel like hitting your head against the wall or jumping out of the window. Thoughts of suicide rise up. You push them down, but they keep returning. You don't want to die, but sometimes you feel as if that would be better than putting up with your own troubled mind. Horrifying as it seems to you, suicide looks sometimes like the only way to rid yourself of your intolerable tensions.

This is the way that most depressions feel, and the fact that, as you say, you've been feeling this kind of tension for several months means that, like many other depressed people, you're caught in a vicious circle. Not only do you feel bad, but you feel bad about feeling bad; the longer the cycle of depression-anger-depression goes on, the worse you feel for letting it go on, and the more intolerant of your self you become.

Right now you probably feel utterly pessimistic about the chances of anyone else—a parent, a friend or a doctor—being able to help you through the nightmare. I know that you must often feel there is no one who really cares about you, who has a handle on your inner torture. Your parents, like most parents, are probably not very good listeners. They are feeling guilty about you, but they don't know how to break through the wall around you. Instead of listening, they preach. They may mean well, but their advice usually comes down to a facile admonition to snap out of it and get down to work. Which only makes you feel worse. Their puritanical, common sense approach to your difficulties might work fine under ordinary circumstances, but when you're depressed it's exactly the wrong approach.

At other times your parents may seem as solicitous and sweet as they are generally harsh and demanding. Trying to overcompensate for being too rough on you, they may sometimes go out of their way to do you little favors, to make your favorite foods, to buy you unexpected presents and generally to protect you by kindness from the trouble you are carrying inside. Naturally this is no more helpful than their demands; it only makes you feel like an overgrown grade-schooler, more helpless than ever before.

Your friends are not much better. They too may mean well when they brush off your problems as insignificant, when they say, 'Come on, forget it. Let's go to a movie.' But they are really no more in touch with your true feelings of fear and resentment than your parents. Their demands that you look on the bright side only reinforce your conviction that they cannot, or will not, penetrate your invisible wall.[22]

Treatment is Advised

All adolescents need a great deal of love and patience. Those who are suffering from depression need even more. If they seem to meet the criteria for depression, parents should seek the help of a physician. Teenagers respond well to antidepressant medication. There are, undoubtedly, a great number of teenagers who have behavioral problems, or who are exhibiting behavior typical of a scared young person trying to find an identity, but I also feel, there are millions of desperate adolescents screaming for help from depression by acting out in unacceptable ways. We need to look beneath the surface behavior, to find out if true depression exists in our children, and then get them the appropriate treatment.

[22] Kiev, Ari, M.D., *Riding Through the Downers*, ((New York: E.P. Dutton, p. 3-6. I highly recommend Dr. Kiev's book to parents, and to teenagers having problems in their family, school or social lives.

CHAPTER SIX
Depression in the Elderly

In the next twenty years the number of people aged 65 to 75 is expected to increase by 23%. The number of those aged 75 and older will increase by 40%.[23] With better standards of living and advances in medical technology today, the average lifespan is increasing. While this, in general, sounds like good news, increased longevity also brings problems for the elderly. They encounter difficult social adjustments. Their children leave home; they are forced to retire; they often move to a new environment, and they can no longer function in society as they used to. They experience emotional hardships as they see close friends pass away, and they witness a new and different generation taking over. There are also many physiologic changes that occur. Eyesight and hearing become impaired, joints ache, and extremeities weaken. They are no longer able to accomplish what they used to and this is manifested by feelings of frustration, anxiety and insecurity.

[23] Federal Council on Aging, "The Need for Long Term Care; Information and Issues," Washington, D.C., U.S. Department of Health and Human Services, DHHS Publ. No. (LHDS)81-20704, 1981.

Often Overlooked and Untreated

With all the added stress that comes with aging, it is no wonder that depression among the elderly is so common. Countless numbers of elderly patients are being treated with multiple drugs for physical manifestations of depression. Thousands of wonderful, otherwise normal elderly patients are considered senile, isolated, forgetful or mean and hateful, just because they are suffering from depression. Bertram Brown, director of the NIMH estimates that half the patients over age 65, who occupy our public mental hospital beds, are suffering from treatable depression which could be lessened or cured completely with proper treatment.[24] Depression in the elderly is a common problem. Although the peak age of depression in women seems to be during child-bearing years, the peak incidence among men seems to occur after the age of 55.

The symptoms of depression are generally the same as those discussed earlier, but some are more or less prominent in different individuals, and all are complicated by other problems of the elderly.

A large number of patients with depression, present themselves initially with physical symptoms such as constipation, malnutrition, or sleep disturbance. These and other common complaints can be interpreted as different types of physical illnesses because there are so many varied illnesses among the elderly and so many side effects possible from their medications. An aging depressed patient may feel overcome with concern for his own body and have constant complaints for which no physical basis can be found.

Depression in the elderly often takes on the appearance of apathy, as he or she withdraws from

[24] Brown, B., Personal document from Fieve: Physicians Guide to Depression, p. 52.

society and refuses to get involved in pleasurable activities. This may occur after the death of a spouse for instance. Then instead of recovering after the normal grieving process withdrawal turns to deep depression. Unfortunately, the apathetic attitude and disinterest in their surroundings, is all too often considered by many, as normal behavior for the aged. This is far from the truth, and is usually a sign of depression.

The decreased appetite, or anorexia, that develops in depression, frequently is a cause of serious malnutrition, muscle wasting, weakness and death. Many lonely older people living alone sit for hours or days without the drive to eat properly, or to even dress and bathe themselves. This is not the normal aging process, but often is a result of depression.

Depression in the elderly is not generally associated with feelings of guilt as it is in younger patients with this malady. It is more often related to loss of self-esteem and feelings of inferiority. The feelings of inadequacy are enhanced by failure to perform physically.

Another contributing factor is the general attitude held by much of the younger population that the older person is weak or inferior, that they are "out of it," and that they are often a burden to their families. These feelings of rejection are magnified greatly by depression.

Loss of mental acuity, confusion or even failing memory are usually considered by family members as part of growing old. Many physicians themselves get trapped into attributing this to "hardening of the arteries," or Alzhiemer's Disease, without first ruling out more readily treated causes such as depression. Often-times there is some degree of underlying disease, but depression worsens it. Abrupt changes, like admission to a hospital or home for the aged, often cause reactive depression and result in mental confusion.

The great medical advances of this century have increased the average life span and allowed people to survive to an older age, but if the mental and emotional changes that come with old age are neglected, then it will be of little benefit to prolong life.

Treatment Offers A Second Chance

There need to be efforts made to recognize depression among the aged, in order to decrease their suffering. Antidepressant treatment in the elderly is successful when symptoms are due to depression. Treatment can restore function, decrease "senility," and promote good nutrition. It will allow thousands of depressed aging people to resume productive lives and feel good about themselves.

CHAPTER SEVEN

SUMMARY

From Devastation to Experiencing the Rewards of Living

My final words are a plea to anyone suffering from symptoms of depression to seek help quickly before it causes further problems in their life.

I also re-emphasize to spouses and family members of those depressed or with PMS that patience and understanding are needed. The person is affected by a chemical imbalance: a real medical illness.

In the future we may have a new name for this illness since depression is not inclusive of all the manifestations of the disease. Some call it a chemical imbalance because so many "chemicals" of the body are adversely affected. Some clinicians now refer to it as Biogenic Amine Deficiency because it describes the lack of catecholamines we have discussed. But regardless of the name, it is comforting to know that the disease has been identified and research will continue to better understand the disease process and how we can best treat it.

I have seen how devastating depression can be to many individuals. I have witnessed relationships and families strained and broken as a result of depression. My sympathy has gone out to those who suffer the awful feelings, understood only by those who have been depressed. I have watched as couples spend the remainder of the month trying to repair their relationship, strained by bitter feelings resulting from premenstrual syndrome. My heart has gone out to those elderly people who sit all alone with the zest for life lost to depression. I have observed the frustration of both parents and children, when adolescent depression causes truancy, delinquency and withdrawal.

Because treatment is so successful, it is imperative that the public be educated in order that depression can be recognized and cured. The average case of untreated depression lasts for about six months, but it may go on for years. If it remains untreated, then the individual has suffered needlessly, and unfortunately, the depressed individual is not the only one to suffer. Spouses and friendships suffer, children suffer, and parents suffer too, as well as bosses and colleagues.

If a person does not have a physician, how does one choose a physician? Although all doctors have at some time in their training learned about depression, not all doctors are interested in diagnosing and treating it. It may be to your advantage to select a physician who has a special interest in it, and who deals with it frequently. Often, word of mouth will help discover a doctor who has successfully treated a number of individuals. As to seeking a specialist, most diagnoses of depression are first recognized by primary care or family practice physicians, just because they are the most likely starting place. However, gynecologists are probably the forerunners in treatment of PMS. It should be recognized that a psychiatrist is a fully trained physician who has specialized in medical problems dealing with mental well-being, and in no way has a negative connotation. There are far too many people with depression and PMS, and too few psychiatrists, but if referred to one by your physician, you should appreciate and respect the experienced knowledge of those in this field of medicine. Whether one seeks help from their family doctor or from a specialist, the correct diagnosis and treatment will usually be made if the physician is approached with "I think I have depression because of this symptom, this symptom and that symptom." It is important to discuss all the symptoms being experienced.

We can be grateful that medical technology has developed a successful treatment for depression. The knowledge of this treatment, must now come to the attention of the public, so that those affected can sooner begin to re-experience the rewards of living, without being handicapped by the disease of depression.

GLOSSARY

adrenal gland: a major gland of the body located near each kidney. This gland, in addition to producing other hormones, is the primary source of norepinephrine or seratonin.

antidepressant: medication used in the treatment of depression. It acts by binding the "reabsorption" of norepinephrine and seratonin so more are available at the nerve synapse for proper message transmission.

anxiety: a feeling of apprehension, fear or uncertainty often accompanied by physiologic changes like fast heartbeat, sweating or tremor. Feelings of anxiety often accompany depression but those that are anxious are not necessarily depressed.

biochemical: the chemical reactions and processes that occur in living organisms. A natural process of the body in performing its function.

biogenic amines: biogenic means produced by living organisms and amines are essential chemical compounds produced by the body from amonia. An example of a biogenic amine is catecholamines.

bipolar depression: a type of depression characterized by highs of euphoria with excessive energy and anxiety alternating with extreme lows found in ordinary depression. These changes may last for hours, days or weeks at a time. It is treated with lithium.

carbohydrate: a major class of food, usually in the form of sugars, starches or celluloses.

catecholamines: chemicals produced largely by the adrenal gland. One type of catecholamine is epinephrine which acts like a stimulant as in the fight or flight response of adrenaline. Two catecholamines important in depression are norepinephrine and seratonin. They act to transmit messages from one nerve to the next and are at low levels in depressed people.

chemical imbalance: the entire body works as a carefully balanced machine. Too much of one compound and not enough of another usually results in an imbalance with a consequence. Too many calories and not enough energy burned results in fat. Not enough insulin results in diabetes. Not enough neurotransmitters results in depression.

cortisol: a hormone produced by the adrenal gland with many functions. The steroid cortisone often injected as an anti-inflammatory, is converted to cortisol in the body. Since it, like catecholamines are produced in the adrenal gland it is easily measured in the blood. It has been used as a possible diagnostic test for depression.

depression: a chemical imbalance due to low levels of catecholamines manifested by symptoms of sleep disturbance, irritability and mood swings, change in appetite, feeling tired, difficulty concentrating, loss of sexual interest, loss of self-esteem, decreased interest in social affairs, physical complaints and a feeling that life is not worth living. Only four or more symptoms present for longer than two weeks severe enough to affect life style are needed for the diagnosis.

dexamethasone: a chemical hormone that plays a role in the regulation of cortisol. One test for depression involves giving dexamethasone to see whether or not it will lower the level of cortisol.

diagnosis: the art of distinguishing one disease from another. A diagnosis can often be made by recognizing the symptoms and by doing an examine. Sometimes different lab tests are needed to confirm the diagnosis. The diagnosis of depression is made by symptoms alone in the majority of cases.

disease: trouble or impairment of the normal state or performance of the body, illness. It is often manifested by characteristic symptoms and may affect the whole body or any of its parts.

dosage: the amount, frequency and size of a given medication

electrochemical: chemical changes produced by electrical action.

electro-convulsive therapy: therapy used by means of electric shock. This form of therapy was more widely used for treatment of depression before the advent of anti-depressant medication. Now it is used only for severe cases not responding to other conventional means of therapy, yet when performed in experienced hands is quite successful and safe.

endogenous depression: depression seemingly coming from within with no apparent outside environmental reason for depression.

estrogen: hormone produced mainly in the ovary of women but also in the adrenal gland and testes which has various functions in both men and women. It is responsible for the female sex characteristics and during the menstrual cycle produces an environment suitable for the implantation of the embryo. As in PMS, altering estrogen levels can lead to many different symptoms and may even have a role in causing depression.

exogenous depression: depression with a cause that seems to originate from external or environmental sources. Depression used to be divided in endogenous or exogenous but now are grouped together as unipolar depression because whether or not there seems to be an outside reason, the symptoms and treatment are the same (at least initially).

fatigue: feeling tired, lack of energy, difficulty performing work due to feeling tired and/or weak.

gastrointestinal disturbances: any or all problems related to the stomach or intestines including stomach ache, cramps, nausea, diarrhea or constipation, vomiting, etc.

gynecologist: a physician specialized in treating the diseases of the genital tract in women. Usually trained in obstetrics as well, which is a specialty in the management of pregnancy, labor and delivery.

hormones: chemicals produced by the body usually by glands which have regulatory affects on different organs of the body. Examples of hormones are estrogen, epinephrine, seratonin and norepinephrine, thyroid, cortisol, insulin etc.

insomnia: difficulty getting to sleep or staying asleep. Sometimes characterized by early morning awakening without getting back to sleep.

lethargy: drowsiness, fatigue or indifference.

lithium: a medication used in the treatment of bipolar depression and experimentally on unipolar depression which has failed conventional therapy.

malady: any sickness, illness or disease.

mania: mental disorder characterized by elation, high emotional state, hyperirritability, excessive talking, increased movements and flight of ideas. This is the 'high phase' in the bipolar manic depressive.

medication: medicine, any drug or remedy designed to alleviate a disease, illness or symptom.

melancholia: a depressed or unhappy emotional state, sadness.

menopause: the stopping of normal menstrual periods in women; usually occurring between the age of 45 and 50. Often times other symptoms occur such as hot flashes and irritability which are probably caused by the imbalance of hormones.

mentation: mental activity. The ability to think and concentrate.

monoamine oxidase inhibitors: a class of drugs used to treat depression. They were among the first medications used successively to treat depression but have largely been replaced by the more effective and safer tricyclic antidepressants.

neurotransmitters: chemicals released at the end of a nerve. These chemicals carry the nerve message across the bridge where two nerves join and stimulate the next nerve to continue with the message. The major neurotransmitter chemicals are two catecholamines called norepinephrine and serotonin. It is insufficient neurotransmitters in the body that is thought to cause depression because there are not enough chemicals to carry across the correct nerve message.

norepinephrine: a chemical produced in the adrenal gland. It is a type of catecholamine and is one of the neurotransmitters lacking in people who have depression.

premenstrual syndrome (P.M.S.): any of multiple symptoms that occur on a cyclic basis around the female menstrual period. Usually symptoms begin a few days to a week before the period and end with its onset. The symptoms possible total over 100 and include such things as depression, irritability, weight gain, tender breasts, headaches, edema — only to mention a few.

progesterone: a hormone produced by the female ovary, adrenal gland or placenta. It serves multiple functions but most commonly noted for preparing the uterus for a fertilized egg and used to stop uterine bleeding.

psychiatrist: a physician who specializes in treatment and prevention of mental illness as well as promoting mental and emotional well being.

psychosis: a general term for any mental disorder whether organic or emotional that is characterized by a deranged personality and loss of contact with reality. There often are hallucinations, delusions or illusions. This would help differentiate true psychosis from chemical depression because one having depression does not have hallucinations and they do recognize reality.

remedy: a medicine or application of something in an attempt to cure a disease or relieve or correct a malady.

self-esteem: this is what one thinks of himself, the way one perceives himself — either for good or bad. Unfortunately, in depression one has a very low self-esteem and this is made worse with the inability to function normally and feeling paranoid about all the symptoms that are beyond control.

serotonin: one of the neurotransmitter catecholamines that serves to transmit messages across the nerve synapse. When this and/or norepinephrine are at low levels in the body, depression is the result.

somatic: pertaining to the body. Somatic complaints are one of the symptoms of depression and the most common include headache, backache and stomachache. Someone with multiple somatic complaints, especially ones that come and go, should be evaluated for depression.

steroid: a group of chemicals produced by the body that include many hormones; each is responsible for various body functions.

stress: a physical, chemical or emotional factor that causes body or mental tension. People react differently to stress. Some get ulcers, others get tension headaches. Even though depression is not directly caused by stress alone it is felt to be a factor in many cases. Often stress can be identified as a causing factor for exogenous depression. Stress is often the cause of anxiety which may or may not be associated with depression.

symptom: a manifestation or evidence of a disease. Symptoms are usually the evidence, change or pain that makes people seek medical help. Unfortunately, in depression, the symptoms are so varied that seldom do people associate these symptoms with depression.

synapse: the gap or junction where two nerves come together. The nerve impulse or message must cross this synapse to reach the other nerve terminal and does so by releasing neurotransmitters which carry the message across the synapse.

treatment: the management or care of a patient for the purpose of combating the disease or disorder. Obviously different treatments are required for different diseases. The standard treatment for chemical depression is tricyclic antidepressants.

tricyclic antidepressants: a group of medicines that are used to treat chemical unipolar depression. They work by blocking the neurotransmitters from being taken up by the body process, allowing more to remain in the nerve synapse to transmit nerve messages. They are safe and non-addicting and essential in the treatment of unipolar depression.

unipolar depression: (see depression) as opposed to bipolar depression where there are ups of manias and downs of depression — unipolar depression has no high manic stages but persistently has four or more of the symptoms of depression.

INDEX

BOOK ORDER FORM

Please send me ________ copies of **DEPRESSION IS CURABLE.**

☐ Enclosed is check or money order for $9.95 each plus $1.50 postage and handling for first copy and 75 cents each additional copy.

☐ Charge to my ☐ VISA ☐ Mastercard

Card No.____________________ Expiration Date ________

____
Name

____
Address

____
City State Zip

RAINBOW PRESS, P. O. Box 855, Clackamas, OR 97015

BOOK ORDER FORM

Please send me ________ copies of **DEPRESSION IS CURABLE.**

☐ Enclosed is check or money order for $9.95 each plus $1.50 postage and handling for first copy and 75 cents each additional copy.

☐ Charge to my ☐ VISA ☐ Mastercard

Card No.____________________ Expiration Date ________

____
Name

____
Address

____
City State Zip

RAINBOW PRESS, P. O. Box 855, Clackamas, OR 97015